OF

SOCIAL LIFE IN WASHINGTON,

BY

MRS. MADELEINE VINTON DAHLGREN.

WASHINGTON, D. C.

1873.

LANCASTER, PA.:
INQUIRER PRINTING AND PUBLISHING COMPANY.
1873.

OF

SOCIAL LIFE IN WASHINGTON.

IF order is Heaven's first law, we should not regard as beneath careful attention, the proper recognition of rules which may tend to avoid confusion in social life.

Because we are a Republic, we are not necessarily to be deprived of those amenities which render life agreeable, and assist to cultivate good feeling.

Courtesy may be considered but as the mirror of charity, and, although it may often become an unmeaning semblance of benevolence, yet, if we assiduously cultivate, if only but the shadow, we may finally hope to gain the reality. Thus, by placing ourselves in excellent relations towards others, we may eventually acquire that sentiment of good will which may at first have been but a mere appearance.

That which is called good breeding is actually the golden rule carried into practice, and is therefore a very Christian accomplishment. Since egotism is the most dreaded bane of society, if we can learn so far to forget ourselves as to consider the just claims of others, we shall have gained a victory over selfishness. But our intention is not to moralize, or present trite truisms, but to place within the scope of a few pages the true state of the present phase of Washington society life.

There are several unsettled questions with regard to which we do not, of course, expect or intend to do more than to indicate, how it seems to us these points may be amicably adjusted.

Washington society life is principally official; or rather, society here is composed, in so great a degree, of official personages, who represent the mechanism of the State, that the social obligations and customs have become about as complex as the constitutional laws upon which the official are based, and yet we have no constitution, or defined code, which makes our social laws as clear as our political. Yet this should be the case.

No reader of history, however superficial his view, but must have noticed how constantly the gravest affairs of State have become complicated with the thousand seeming nothings of every-day life. Nor have we been at all exempt from such entanglements. On the contrary, every one at all familiar with the past social incidents of Washington, is perfectly aware of various occasions in which animosities have been engendered by the omission, or the commission, of certain requirements, exacted by some, and not so understood by others. It is, indeed, extraordinary, that this subject has not compelled a more explicit understanding, long ago, in view of the many embarrassments, and some of them not unimportant, that have already arisen from alternate neglect or ignorance of social observances, which, in order to avoid confusion, should be well understood and carefully weighed.

Nor can ignorance of the official etiquette prevailing here, be construed into any want of general society training elsewhere, because we have in Washington a very exceptional basis.

When the Republic was first organized, we all know that the venerated Washington and his stately wife, compelled a rigid observance of social etiquette towards the administration in its various branches. General Jackson, when he became President, first broke down the barriers of careful respect, and received all comers without any formal or special rules; and the consequence was, that a disorder and rudeness characterized those receptions hitherto unknown, and which no private gentleman in the country would have tolerated in his own home.

If our staunch republicanism renders us unwilling to acknowledge that the President and his wife are the "first gentleman and lady" of the land, yet we may assuredly, without danger to our social independence, accord them socially that respectful deference which the Constitution gives to the Executive in the exercise of his granted prerogatives. Beginning here, we may well concede to the various Departments that social recognition which is in harmony with the Constitution.

Not a winter passes but we hear the same questions asked over and over again, by scores of persons entering, for the first time, into public life, or by strangers, who come here to participate in our social festivities, who do not know what are the peculiar social requirements the official element has introduced. We may justly commence our remarks upon these peculiar exigencies, by a consideration of the position of the Presidential family.

The President, as the executive head of the nation, is properly entitled to precedence. This first place is, of course, accorded to him, whenever and wherever he appears in social life. His social privileges entitle him to receive all calls, without being expected to return any. In conversation, he is addressed as "Mr. President." Some choose to use the phrase "Your Excellency," but, we believe, this is a matter of taste only. The present usage does not require any special preliminary formalities, in order to make the acquaintance of the President. During the session of Congress, he gives stated receptions, and all persons who desire do so may attend these levees. Upon entrance, you give your name to an usher, and are announced. You are, thereupon, introduced to the President by the Marshal of the District, or, at times, by some other person who may have been designated for such purpose, and you are immediately after presented to the different members of the Presidential family, who may be present.

In case you are precise, you leave your card before your

departure from the Executive Mansion. If the reception is held in the morning, the usual costume for morning receptions suffices. If in the evening, a full toilette is demanded. It is not respectful to appear in less than evening dress, at an evening reception given by the President. Even in making an evening call, at any time, it is more proper to make at least a demi-toilette. Those ladies who are fastidious, do not wear a bonnet in making an evening visit at the President's. We have seen the wives of Foreign Ministers call in full evening dress. If the President have a wife, she also receives the first visit from every one, nor is she expected to return any. Of course, if she desires to be especially kind, she is at liberty to make visits, although we believe it has been found a safer rule not to make distinctions. But other members of the Presidential family are allowed by custom to return visits, and acknowledge civilities tendered. At the state dinners of the President the usual etiquette prevails, as at other dinner tables where official personages are entertained.

It is not permissible to decline a dinner, or other invitation of a social nature, sent by the President, unless in case of your own illness, or of that of any member of your family, or of the death of a relative. When, however, it is imperative to send a regret, explain in your note the reasons which compel a non-acceptance. Indeed, it is more respectful to state the cause, rather than to send a merely formal regret, whenever an excuse of sufficient gravity may be assigned; so that it may plainly appear that your absence is unavoidable. This may also apply to other invitations, which you desire to treat with especial consideration. Any invitation of a social nature, extended by the President of the United States, must be considered, by courtesy, as a command; and, therefore, it is allowable to waive all other previous engagements made, which may conflict with your acceptance—even if it happen to be a dinner. But in no other instance may an invitation to dine, once accepted, be revoked; and even in such case you should mention the nature of the obligation which compels you.

The President is to be addressed, in writing, as "His Excellency, the President of the United States." The various members of the Cabinet, respectively, as "The Honorable, the Secretary of State," "The Honorable, the Secretary of the Treasury," "The Honorable, the Secretary of War," "The Honorable, the Secretary of the Navy," "The Honorable, the Secretary of the Interior," "The Honorable, the Postmaster-General," and "The Honorable, the Attorney-General." The Vice-President, and the Chief Justice, simply as such. Do not abbreviate words in sending a ceremonious note. When an official title, as in the case of Diplomatic functionaries, is very long, whatever portion of the prefix you give, use the entire word, and then add "&c., &c.," in an under line, which is supposed to include all that is claimed. All abbreviations are in bad taste in formal notes, whatever may be the title, whether civic, military, or naval. The word "Present," written on an envelope, formerly much used, is now quite obsolete, except as confined to communications of a business nature, such as bills sent, and the French words "*En Ville*" have superseded its use. Although we are decidedly opposed to the introduction of Gallicisms, as likely to emasculate the vigorous Saxon of our noble language, yet in matters of polite usage we may well continue to imitate our ancestors, and introduce the courtly Norman phrases—they so aptly turn aside the blunt edge of much that is disagreeable in this busy, material life we lead. But we do object to that hybrid term, the "*Republican Court*," which we so often hear. It is senseless, and an anomaly; or if it have a meaning, it is still more to be deprecated, as incompatible with the spirit of the framers of our excellent Constitution. We have no "Court circle," nor do we expect to remain a Republic and at the same time ape "Court" manners. We have a social, as well as a political autonomy. Let us preserve these with an equal jealous care and dignity. Our official etiquette is not intended as a personal compliment, but addresses itself to the office borne, so that it remains strictly in harmony with our Republican sentiments. When the incumbent loses office, he becomes again simply a private citizen, whom the Republic has honored. This is such a very beautiful provision of our legal Constitution, that we should never lose sight of its bearing on social life and manners. It is the counteracting and saving element, as opposed to all hereditary distinction, and holds each man and woman intact in the exercise of those talents by which he or she may regulate the individual destiny. The very words "Republican Court" have a fatal sound of Cæsarism; and, as we have already remarked, words become facts—they are the expression of the soul's aspirations. We should prove to the world that Republican manners are the very acme of true elegance, in their unaffected simplicity.

It has always been, and still remains a matter of discussion, as to whom properly belongs the second place in social precedence, and equally accomplished persons differ on this point. This position is claimed for both the Chief Justice and the Vice President, and so many good reasons may be given on either side, that until a social congress can be convened to decide this, and some other controverted points, there can be no decision attained. It seems to us, however, that the Chief Justice exercises functions of such sacred importance, and of such a nature, that the second place should be given to him. He presides over the tribunal of ultimate appeal, he holds his office for life, he is placed beyond all the mutations incident to most other officials, however exalted. We have only to read the Constitution of the United States to be impressed with the immense dignity of his position. The same immutability characterizes the functions of the other Justices of the Supreme Court, who hold their position for life, and are placed on a higher plane, above the political excitements of the country. These gentlemen are to be respectively addressed in conversation as Mr. Chief Justice, and as Mr. Justice; and it has been usual to accord them precedence over Cabinet Ministers and Senators—for at times they may exercise a controlling influence over the Executive. At least, we have seen this precedence given, although we can recall, in our earlier life, some bitter feuds on this score, between the wives of Court and Cabinet dignitaries, and we never yet remember to have heard of a feminine warrior retreating, when she once was committed to open battle. So these ladies may have left a legacy of contested honors, to those who came after them. If so, in the name of Heaven's first law, let us have peace.

If, then, for we tread on shaking ground, these Justices walk in their silken robes so high, why not give the Chief Justice precedence over the Vice-President? And this we venture to suggest, without any derogation to the exalted position of the Vice-President, whose chief dignity arises from his being president of the U. S. Senate—for, as Vice-President simply, he has no cares, no especial duties, no political significance. His political importance is rather anticipatory than actual. Yet, we must say, that we would only rather avoid this difficulty at our own table, by being careful not to invite these two high dignitaries to meet at the same time.

Succeeding the President, the Vice-President, the Chief-Justice, comes the Speaker of the House, who, as well as the Vice-President, is a possible successor to the Presidency, and although he may be, and generally is, a political power of the first importance, yet, socially, he comes in the fourth place. He is addressed, in conversation, as "Mr. Speaker." All these gentlemen we have mentioned, receive the first visit from all others.

The General of the Army, and the Admiral of the Navy, occupy very exceptional positions. They fill stations made for them by a grateful country, in recognition of special services, and the rank they hold has been bestowed upon them for life. Yet, properly speaking, they leave no successors, except as the roll of fame shall proclaim these trumpet-tongued to the nation. As to the social precedence their rank entitles them to, inasmuch as they move, as it were, in eccentric orbits, they may be allowed the brilliant revolutions of luminaries which appear in the heavens, and disappear without interruption to the general plan—in plain words, they are special creations, and not an essential part of the machinery of the State, and leave no successors to their places. We believe they come after the four classes of officials we have mentioned, and, we suppose, relatively to each other, according to the order of the creation of the Army and Navy Departments by the Government. This rank, it seems to us, is theirs by right and not by courtesy alone, as the General of the Army, and the Admiral of the Navy, represent the two arms of the Government, through whom it must act directly, in case of war. Some are of opinion, that these special creations should hold social positions of precedence subordinate to the Cabinet, and to the Senate. Regarding this, we would ask: To what dizzy height may the Senate, expressing the acclaim of the nation, and vested with the confirming power by the Constitution, raise those whom they delight to honor? Does this august body take these patriotic defenders of the Republic, from the gates of the Temple of Janus, which these heroes have closed, invest them with titles as with a shining raiment, and, at the same moment limit *their own power* of conferring this lustre of renown? Does not the very precedence, which may be thus assigned them—this place set apart by common consent, as in the case of the Chief Magistracy—present the utmost possible inducement the country may offer, to stimulate military and naval achievement? Nor can the Senate be less in honor, when it thus assists to build so high the bulwarks of the Executive in time of war; and it must not be overlooked, as we have already said, that no general rule can become established here —for, at the death of the incumbents, the station disappears. It will then anew require the Promethean spark of *genius aiding opportunity*, to revive the rank. Until such time may again come, the Army and Navy will once more be commanded by the Senior Officer of the service, and routine resuming its sway, the old place under the respective Departments will be assigned. Among officers of the Army and Navy there exists a corresponding rank—the Lieutenant-General and the Vice-Admiral—the Major-General and the Rear-Admiral—the Brigadier-General and the Commodore—the Colonel of the Army relatively to the Captain of the Navy—and so on *pari passu*. Upon this rule a social precedence can alone be placed, whenever formal or ceremonious occasions require it.

We have now to consider the Cabinet—and here we must remark, that so much confusion at once appears, as really to make the whole subject a discouraging one.

As to the Cabinet, relatively to each other, the order observed is that priority in which these offices were created—thus: the State, the Treasury, the War, the Navy, the General Post-office, the Interior, and the Department of Justice. The Chiefs of these Departments, form the Executive Council of the Administration, but at the same time they are actual Heads of Departments of State. These functionaries alike expect to receive calls, and alike claim the same privileges, and it is only upon State occasions, such as official receptions, or formal State dinners, or other state ceremonials, that their order need be specially defined. Yet these situations are of not unfrequent occurrence, and no embarrassment should arise when they do present themselves.

It has been a contested point, as to who should pay the first visit upon each other—the Cabinet officer or the Senator—but there would seem to be a growing tendency to yield to the Senatorial claim. This claim is based on the argument that the Senator represents State sovereignty, and that the dignity is, consequently, superior to that of the Cabinet officer, whose nomination the Senate confirms by its vote, and who is appointed Constitutional aid and adviser of the President Yet, the Cabinet officer is something more than this; for, presiding over an entire Department of the Government, he possesses both power and dignity of function. As to his confirmation being subject to the vote of the Senate, the Senator, in turn, is subject to the State legislature for his appointment, and this line of reasoning would place a State Senator above a United States Senator, and the Great Unwashed above the State Senator. Evidently, we cannot go back to first principles too closely in a Republic, in order to regulate our ceremonial.

But we do not propose to enter the domain of Constitutional law, but simply to explain points, some established and others controverted, of social law, and give reasons, where any exist, for certain customs.

To our apprehension, leaving grave Cabinet Ministers and Senators to arrange questions of relative social importance, or rather their wives to do this for them—for it is women who are social agitators in the Republic—we really think that Senators' wives might safely yield this point to the Cabinet, when all the circumstances are considered; or if this cannot be effected, at least let a compromise be made, that certain *privileges* are to be accorded by courtesy, still to be held in reserve as a *right*.

The ladies of the Cabinet have literally the public at their doors, and no one woman can possibly have health, strength and endurance, to enable her to meet the heavy burden imposed. These ladies are few in number—their residence here is fixed, central and well known; while the families of Senators often come here for a short period of time only, and unless they call in person, or send their card giving their address, the utmost vigilance may not detect their momentary presence. It is true that many Senators have permanent residences here also, and even live in a superior style to Cabinet officers, yet we now speak of the general rule. The rapidly increasing size of our society, really demands that there should be some exemption allowed by custom to the higher officers of the executive, with regard to the personal notice of visits. If it were once understood, that to return a call by a card sent, and afterward acknowledge the visit received (in all cases where the person who calls has any social claims that are recognized in general society), by cards of invitation to receptions, these ladies would then be allowed some respite. To return a thousand visits in person, is a hardship none can realize except those who have attempted the task. And moreover it becomes an utterly senseless formality. Why are these calls made by society in general? They are made as a mark of respect for the elevated station, and also in order to participate in the receptions which these functionaries give, from time to time. These objects could be better met, if it were permissible to send cards in recognition of visits, and if where personal visits were made, the exceptions simply included, the Supreme Court, the U. S. Senate, the Diplomatic

Body, the General and the Admiral, while outside of these functionaries, an exception was allowed; and if *this rule* were once established, no invidious comments could be made. That which renders it so very disagreeable *now* to receive a card in place of a personal visit, is the knowledge that your call is not treated with the same respect that is paid to that of others; but a general rule could not produce ill-feeling. We see this notably in the case of the President and his wife. No one feels aggrieved because his or her visit is in no manner returned by these personages.

Again, the card receptions that Cabinet Ministers find it incumbent to give, are of necessity so large that they are unpleasantly crowded for both host and guest. Why not select some suitable public hall for these receptions, and let each Cabinet Minister hold therein one, two or more card receptions, during what is called "the season." We know of no social experience so disagreeable, as to make one of a dense mass of human beings, literally packed into rooms of ordinary dimensions. It forms no compensation, that it is the "polite world," that suffocates you! Let any one, philosophically or cynically disposed, gain, if he can, a few inches of space in a corner, and become a spectator of such scenes as occur every winter at our crowded receptions; and the sheer absurdity of calling this aggregation, social life, becomes at once apparent. It is rather to be wondered at, that dreadful accidents have not before now recalled society to its senses in this matter. We have entered many a hospitable door, and looking upward beheld such a surging mass of human beings on the stairway, that, dismayed at the idea of wedging ourselves into this fearful crowd, we have sent our wraps back into the carriage from the door, rather than attempt to gain the dressing room; and only venturing far enough to pay our respects to the beleaguered host and hostess, have made a speedy exit—society, conversation, beauty of effect, were all lost, all rendered impossible through want of space.

And this evil will go on increasing, unless some changes are effected. The same controversy, as to the first visit, which implies precedence, has also existed as regards the Diplomatic body, who represent other countries near our own. We have known some ladies of the Senate who have refrained from making the first visit upon the wives of Foreign Ministers, assigning the same reason, that the Senators represented a State sovereignty, while the Minister was only an accredited functionary from a foreign power—it being held that the Ambassador or Envoy alone properly represented the sovereignty of a State, and this rank is not often sent to us. Yet the Minister Plenipotentiary and Envoy Extraordinary certainly has a special mission, and may be said to represent State sovereignty, if not the person of the sovereign. This of course involves the question of relative dignity, and this in turn involves a veritable treatise on international law, and places the whole subject beyond the patience of our feminine disputants. We would make the womanly appeal in behalf of the foreigner, *of courtesy to the stranger.* Based upon this sentiment, which should dominate us in their case, we would grant a Foreign Minister precedence, wherever it can at all be given. This precedence relatively to each other, rank being equal, is accorded to priority of residence among us. The *Dean* or *Doyen* enters upon his functions in virtue of length of stay near our government. Yet we have witnessed very grave offense given at a dinner table, where the host led in the wife of a Foreign Minister, the fair belligerent being the wife of a Senator who claimed the honor as her due.

Now, since it is to be presumed that the special object of every entertainment is, to promote good-will and not to foster ill-will, it is to be regretted that no definite rule as regards social official classification prevails. A carefully adjusted ceremonial would be no more incompatible with Republican institutions than the legal classification which now exists, and which must continue to endure. These have a fixedness co-existent with the Republic, and our social life is their complement. Let us not undervalue its importance. Daniel Webster called a well-appointed dinner "the climax of civilization." We ought to be able to reach this climax smoothly. The morning call, the breakfast, the luncheon, the "*matinée dansante*," the *musicale*, the *soirée* conversational, and the assembly, are all and each charming in their degree as adjuncts of social life; yet, the dinner is "*the climax.*"

Now, there are some dinner rules which are absolute, although we fear at times they are either misunderstood, or at all events disregarded. It seems needless to recapitulate, and yet the very fact that mistakes are so often made, must serve as our apology here. For instance, an invitation to dine must be precise, and should be couched in some such formula as the following:

MR. JONES

REQUESTS THE HONOR OF

MR. SMITH'S

COMPANY AT DINNER,

On Monday, the 1st December, at 7 o'clock.

Nov. 22, '73. R. S. V. P.

When such an invitation is received, an answer should not only be given in writing, but it should be sent at the very earliest moment at all practicable.

We knew a diplomat here, renowned for courtly manners, and for the incomparable dinners which he gave, whose answer to a dinner invitation came on one occasion so promptly, that our own messenger, who also returned to us quickly, had not reached the house, when the acceptance arrived. And the fine point on this piece of good manners was, that this was an acceptance, too—not a regret, which is considered to demand greater expedition, even, in the sending. This gentleman entertained his friends so constantly at dinner, that he understood the importance of prompt attention. In writing an answer to a formal dinner invitation, we should be careful to make it as exact as the note we have received. Indeed, we should repeat this note. Our host has a title—for instance,

The President—repeat his title just as he himself may indicate to you. In answer to Mr. Jones, you reply:

MR. SMITH

HAS THE HONOR TO ACCEPT

MR. JONES'

POLITE INVITATION TO DINNER,

For Monday, the 1st December, at 7 o'clock.

Nov. 22, '73.

The reason for this repetition is to show that you have perfectly comprehended the invitation, so that no error may have been committed, as to time or place. We have known awkward mistakes to occur from want of attention in this matter.

Then, again, there should be no possibility of mistake as to your acceptance, or non-acceptance. Let your answer be positively, "Yes," or "No." At any other entertainment we may perhaps avail ourselves of a reasonable uncertainty, but not so with the dinner.

We once knew a poor little lady, "on hospitable thoughts intent," who went to live in a small town in the west. She had been accustomed to the well-regulated dinner at home, and had been taught to consider that the highest form of compliment, was to ask a friend to dinner. Wishing to be on the best terms with her new neighbors, she sent out the usual written cards of invitation to a score of guests—a formidable undertaking in a country village—but she was nothing daunted, and all the preparations went on bravely. Nothing was wanting to make her dinner a success, but the dreadful fact that, up to the very last moment, she remained uncertain as to the number of her guests. In reply to her written invitations, came a score of *verbal* messages, such as "They *hoped* to come;" "Would come if they could;" "Could not tell *exactly* if their engagements would permit;" "If well enough would come." But in no one case was a positive response received. So the banquet had to be prepared on this score. The hour came and passed, and after a famishing delay, which spoiled everything—two tardy guests dropped straggling in—and four rueful people sat down to a superb dinner prepared for twenty covers. This actually took place.

This grand collapse is just what may be expected, where no one knows his own intentions, and society would receive its final doom did such conditions widely exist. Yet, very disagreeable complications have arisen, even in Washington, from not paying due attention to the importance of a *definite answer*. Suppose, for example, there are *fourteen* covers at your dinner—and fourteen forms a pleasant and a favorite number, suiting very well the size of the home dining-room ordinarily. Let fourteen be all counted, and suppose one guest disappoints! He leaves *thirteen* miserable souls, to tell ghost stories, and wonder if the dinner will poison them; which very likely it may do, since they were all so "blue" in the discussing of it. It must be remembered that the guests at a dinner table, must be properly placed in advance, each plate marked with the name of the expected guest written on a card, or on the *menu*, or bill of fare, and the *dinner chart* mapped out, as if by line and compass, so as to avoid all these sunken rocks and breakers we have been considering, so as to place people who will like each other in proximity, so as to give "honor where honor is due," so as to keep husband and wife from treading on each other's toes, so as to please those you entertain, by giving widows and marriageable young ladies desirable "*partis*" to captivate, so as to put the old decanter of old Madeira near the *bon-vivant*, so as to leave the ends of your table open and unoccupied, and the central places filled with your most distinguished officials! Now, how is all this, and more too, to be done—pleasure to reign, confusion to be avoided, exact distribution of this cornucopia of blessings to be showered on your blissful guests, unless there is *certainty*.

Is not life miserable, because of the uncertainty of all its enjoyments, and are we thus ever to be cheated of even momentary happiness? A thousand times—say yes or no—and let the pleasure of this supreme social gratification be unimpaired!

The length of time preceding the dinner invitation, marks the degree of formality which it is expected will characterize the arrangements. A card of invitation sent ten days in advance, informs us of a state dinner. Eight days of notification is the usual time; after that, even four or five days may be allowed, as simply inviting to a social dinner, or even two or three days, if "*en petit comité.*" We once had the honor to be "one of seven" at such a dinner, where Seward, Stanton and a foreign celebrity were entertained by a diplomat—the short stay in the city of the guest of the occasion, whom we were invited to meet, being the reason mentioned for the hurried summons. But the informal dinner is rather the privilege of private life, and we are now considering the official etiquette of Washington, where State functionaries are expected to invite eight days in advance. To allow so much time is certainly the highest compliment, since it more surely secures the original number selected. The time designated having arrived, *punctuality* is imperative. Dinner rules do not allow over fifteen, or at the most twenty minutes of delay, in order to await the arrival of any guest, no matter how exalted his functions in the State may be. Courtesy to those present requires that you give the company assembled their dinner before it spoils or grows cold. So pray arrive, if you can, at the precise moment at which you are invited. If you reach the house the first guest at a dinner, in place of waiting until some one else shall appear, rather pride yourself upon your superior good breeding for the nonce, and enter at once. Ladies attend formal dinners "en grande toilette," and gentlemen in the corresponding and conventional dress suit of black, with white "choker"—only, messieurs, do not wear *white* gloves; take lavender or any delicate tint in preference. At times, officers of the army or navy prefer to show their respect by wearing uniforms; and we love this dress so well—

it appeals so gratefully to our patriotism—that we are always glad to see it. Yet senior officers especially, having been "in harness," as these old "war-horses" call it, all their lives, are not sorry to get out of the constraint, and wear the dress suit of black also. However, if the occasion is one of state, this will scarcely be permitted. Gloves must be worn upon entrance to the drawing-room, but must always be taken off at the moment one is seated at the table. A recent innovation, which, if the fashionable world could suspect was *an economy*, would probably be at once scouted—but which we like *any way*—permits that the gloves shall not be replaced at all, after their removal at the table. This, however, may be only one of those flitting fashions worn like the glove for the moment, and then cast aside. Yet, do not forget that during the serving of a dinner, the waiters in attendance *alone* wear gloves! And even the waiter, serves with greater elegance, with the thumb of the hand wrapped in a damask napkin. Previous to the announcement, that "dinner is served," the host informs each gentleman which lady he is expected to lead in to dinner, and introduces them to each other, in case they happen not to be acquainted. Indeed, we think at a dinner of moderate size, the *convives* should all know each other, and should be introduced, if need be, by the host. Dinner announced, the host offers his left arm to the lady who has the highest official position present, and the hostess leaves the drawing-room last, led in by the gentleman of the first official distinction present. We once knew of a lawless old diplomat, who *would* lead in with the prettiest young girl of the company, at his own splendid dinners; but his demoralizing course met that grave reprobation it deserved from all virtuous matrons! As a just punishment for such discreditable conduct, he fell a victim finally to an innocent and confiding young creature of seventeen, left the country, and took his American bride to his foreign home, where he lives doubtless a reformed man, if indeed he still survive!

Thus our polite host and hostess, take the central seats opposite to each other, being supported on either side by their most distinguished guests. The reason the extreme ends of a table should be left open, no seats placed there if possible, and at all events never occupied by the entertainers, is very obvious; since from a central position one can better care for one's guests, and promote conversation and a genial and measured degree of hilarity; while on the other hand, if guests are given the extreme ends, it may seem to place them "below the salt." As to the suitable service of a table, Washington has many good caterers and intelligent waiters, whose attendance can readily be procured, in case the home establishment needs to be reinforced—as indeed it generally does, in order to meet the requirements of a banquet. So, the chief care of the host and hostess, should be to forget that the dinner is being served, and try to interest their guests. As to the *menu*, or bill of fare, which it is better to put at each plate, for the information of the epicurean appetite, we would suggest not to yield implicitly to the caterer, who will be sure to prolong your dinner beyond the bounds of good taste. Especially should this be the case, where a sudden acquisition of fortune gives hospitable people the means of entertaining. Such persons, quite unaccustomed to judge for themselves of what is really proper, are readily imposed upon by those whose interest it is to provide lavish feasts. A banquet must be sumptuous rather in the careful choice and quality, than in the profuse quantity of the selected dishes. If you desire to spend money without stint when giving dinners, do so rather by the artistic elaboration of that which you present, than by an endless repetition of courses which pall upon the taste. Do not be persuaded to exceed ten courses—it is wearisome; let the wines be delicate, and do not mix wines in which tastes conflict. The French custom (and the French are unrivalled in all matters of taste) of only presenting each wine once, is excellent; it effectually prevents all inebriating excess, which is so utterly disgraceful, if it happen to occur.

A very great reform, however, has taken place in the past few years with regard to the use of wines. Doubtless the agitation kept up by temperance societies has had something to do with this; but much also has been effected by the happy introduction of light native wines amongst us, at moderate prices. When the *vin-du-pays* becomes as cheap here as it is in France and Italy, we shall have effectually swept away the intoxicating poisons which as yet are demanded. We recollect hearing our father, the Hon. S. F. Vinton, say that when he came here in 1823, the then youngest member of the House and a bachelor, he absolutely dreaded a dinner, on account of the social tyranny in the matter of drinking. Old English customs then prevailed at the dinner, and the calibre of a man's brain was measured at dinner by the capacity of his stomach to guzzle bumpers. For a man of exceedingly delicate nerve organization, such as our own dear father had, who considered a clear head as absolutely needful for a wise legislator, this custom was torture. Let us rejoice that this enforced dissipation has given way to more Christian ideas. If we could only, when we exercise hospitality, learn to set aside such lavish luxury as sinful, and share with the poor of the Lord, by dividing this excess somewhat with them, we would in this way, if only in an imperfect degree, obey the injunction to call in from the highways and the by-ways the suffering multitude. As we write of costly banquets our pen falters, and tearful visions of pale faces, and of starving children, rise before us. As a Christian woman, and as we hope for mercy hereafter for ourselves, we can but implore society, to let the crumbs that fall from its table, console the Lazarus at its door. A winter of unusual hardship for these little children of our common Father is anticipated, and we wish some united action could be had to avoid waste. But we turn our saddened eyes from the cold, and chill, and hungry gaze without, to the light and warmth, and glow within, and we again ask our pleasant hostess not to be afraid of exercising her own individual taste, in the matter of adornment of her table. An original thought, if it is graceful, pleases the old diner-out, who wearies of the monotony of conventional elegance. It is too tiresome to see the same hired ornaments day after day, and to go through the same unvarying routine. Rather use a simple vase of flowers, than a piece of finery hired for the occasion. Personal care bestowed, is more flattering than the hired glitter. We once said to our hostess, "You have produced a fine effect," when we were shocked by the disclaimer, "And yet we took no pains!" Now, it was for this very "pains," for the thoughtful care to please, we were thanking her!

Our dinner-talk is over, the hostess rises first, and all proceed to the drawing room, where coffee, the *demi-tasse*, cordials, and an hour later tea, are served. The hostess usually serves the tea herself, but this is not *de rigueur*, and although we love to see a hostess exercise "*les petits soins*"—those little acts of hospitable care—yet we confess to being most bent upon conversation, and to our dislike of anything that interrupts the "flow of reason and the feast of soul." The after dinner hour is precious in its genial exercise of intellect, or for music. At such times a gracious play of fancy is stimulated, and even the cup of tea should be used "to cheer," and not to interfere. Yet many a gentle dame presides so gracefully at the tea-board, and dispenses the grateful beverage with such pleasant words, that none may cavil. We have in our eye now, one of our most honored matrons, her placid face almost hidden by the burnished silver, the hissing tea-urn, the snowy bowl of sugar, and as she handles the quaint old china, we hear her say: "For twenty-five years have I made tea, seated just here, at this board"—just twenty-five years! and "*here*," then, the monarchs of thought, who have toiled to bring about the culmination of our nation's grandeur, have sipped their Bohea! The "old families" of Washington have an interest for us, which none other in the land may claim, for their social life has gone hand in hand with that of the nation. But we have not yet bade our hostess adieu, a formality we may dispense with at a *soirée*, but not at a dinner.

The gentlemen, some of them, are still in the smoking-room. We feel sorry that they smoke so long, for charming women are here, and it is the common loss. Perhaps, like social cowards, they retreat from an apprehended captivity.

We are at liberty to leave after the coffee, but we linger still and sip our tea. However, during what is called the season, social festivities become so multiplied, that one may have several engagements to meet later than the dinner. It is therefore admissible to leave as soon as the coffee is handed. Succeeding the dinner, a visit which the French wittily call *visite-de-digestion* must be made within the week.

Precedence at the dinner table is the grand subject of social wrangling in Washington, and the need of a fixed rule is here so painfully apparent, that those who have been taught to be careful by sad experience, will simply avoid asking those functionaries to meet each other whose claims may conflict. Yet the Vice President, the Chief Justice, the Speaker, the General of the Army, the Admiral of the Navy, Foreign Ministers, Cabinet Ministers and Senators, they and their wives ought to be able to meet, and dine in peace together! Let a social congress or woman's parliament be convened, composed of these ladies, where, after all the arguments and respective claims have been duly weighed, some positive rules may be agreed upon. It is surprising what *natural aristocrats* women are. In the army and navy, for example, the wives of officers adhere more rigidly to designated and relative social rank, than the officers do themselves; nor do our American women object to bear foreign titles of distinction. Indeed, in this they reason wisely; for in countries where class distinctions exist, these usually imply respectable lineage.

We would here remark, that Cabinet officers are addressed as "Mr. Secretary." We do not like this, for it designates the lowest rather than the highest functions which these officials fill. They are in one sense "Secretaries" of the President, appointed by the Executive Head and confirmed by the U. S. Senate; but at the same time they are active, if not responsible heads of vast departments of the government, with a power, patronage and influence, which, if it were permanent, would exceed that of many petty potentates of other countries. *Names become things* in history, and we believe if "Mr. Secretary" were changed to "Mr. Minister," "The Premier," and so on, it would help to adjust the matter of social precedence.

Senators are addressed as "Mr. Senator," and this is as it should be. Members of the House of Representatives are introduced as the "Honorable Mr." but simply addressed in conversation as "Mr." that is, if a plain Mister can be found in that popular body. But we venture to say, from an intimate knowledge of our rural districts, that every man of them bears *a title* at home. He is "Squire," "Judge," "Captain," "Colonel," "General," and so through all the gamut of the key-board of possible or impossible prefixes! The republic seems to avenge itself for having made the permanency of families unattainable, by piling Pelion upon Ossa, during a man's natural life! And now come women who claim to be Miss Doctor, and Mrs. Reverend, on their own account!

With regard to women's titles, it is becoming more and more the custom to say "Mrs. Secretary," "Mrs. Senator," "Mrs. General," "Mrs. Admiral," and so on. They do this in Europe to be sure, so that it cannot be laughed at as ridiculous. Yet, since we are a Republic, we are supposed to stand on the basis of personal merit, and distinction won for ourselves. But, perhaps, when a woman captures a President or other dignitary, she has won the right to claim the title too. Some are said to "wear the breeches," "rule the roast," be the "better half," and "captain of the ship." From our own observation at the Capital of this great nation, something more of substance than the empty title, is wielded by the women who represent the country here. And we should be very sorry to see our fair and very able sisters, disturbed in their privileges and right womanly prerogatives. How much nicer for example to be the wife of a President, than to be Mr. President; for as it is, one has a good share of the power, and none of the responsibility. But of course we don't mean exactly what we say: women often do not. We think, however, that while it may be in good taste, to give a lady these titular distinctions, held really by their husbands, yet it would be in bad taste to use them for one's self. Certainly it is very convenient, when introducing ladies, to give such nominal rank as may at once clearly and distinctly designate them in the very fact of introduction. It would often save a long explanation, or an uncertainty still more disagreeable.

Members of the House of Representatives and their wives, are expected to make the first visit upon all the classes of functionaries we have mentioned; but citizens of Washington, and those in private life, owe them in turn the first visit.

There is a territorial government in this city, but as it is of very recent date, we really can form no idea of what its social claims may be; but it seems to us, as compared to the National Government, it must stand as a separate creation, and take a subordinate position. Perhaps the Governor's office may be exceptional to this rule; yet, inasmuch as governors of territories have never appeared in Washington society to any extent, but remained in their far-off homes, we are again at a loss.

If this territorial government continue in existence, those who write on this theme ten years hence will be able to judge better. Yet, thus far, everything connected with the management of this district, has been subject to so various change, that we can only exclaim, *omne principium grave!*

The citizens of Washington form among themselves, outside of the consideration of official life, a body of society, to be regulated by the same rules which dominate other societies; yet as we have said before, Washington life is essentially official life, and we can scarcely separate the two.

When you attend a reception, do not omit to leave your card with the usher in the hall. In some houses it is the custom always to give your name to the usher, who then announces you *a haute voix*. Of course, in a society where so many strangers meet, and which is so cosmopolitan in its nature, it may often be essential to announce in this way. In public receptions, it is entirely so; but we must enter a protest against the awkward usher, who murders your name outright, cuts you into halves and shows you no quarters. As to those foreigners who have a quartering to their names, they must be fearful sufferers! Let the usher be well trained to announce, or dispense with his services in this respect altogether, as an unmitigated nuisance. A gentleman of distinction once came into our presence with a sigh of relief as we greeted him by the well-known cognomen.

"How good it is," said he, "to hear my name once more. I began to be uncertain as to my own identity."

We laugh, and ask what he means? "Well, simply this: I have been attending receptions all the morning, and have heard my name so mangled by the ushers, and have found myself repeated under so many different titles, that I am bewildered."

Use a plain card, if you do not wish to be supposed fanciful, and never have it printed. Great men, whose autographs are precious, confer a favor certainly by writing the name on the card, but it is more convenient and more elegant for society in general, to have the name engraved on the card. It is also very comfortable for old ladies, who read through glasses, if these letters are plain and legible.

The clergy take a signal position, and we think should always be accorded *the* place of honor when present in society. They are the Envoys of a Higher Power, and have the most important and sacred mission of all. We were once at a dinner where a clergyman was present, and there were Foreign Ministers and Cabinet Ministers, Senators and others of dignity, when the venerable *Doyen* of the Corps Diplomatique, asked the hostess to assign the place at her side for which he had been designated, to the clergyman. And this wise old gentleman, who understood so well all matters of social courtesy, decided on true principles, based upon that Divine law which is above human law, and goes beyond it.

Very aged persons, also, should be treated with peculiar respect. God has stamped upon them the majesty of years, and we must give them a deferential place. At this moment, the nation beholds a touching example of filial respect in the family of its Chief Magistrate; and it seems to us a Providential spectacle, at a time when insubordination to parents, is a growing evil throughout the land. Many years since, a friend of ours, the wife of a public man, was led in to dinner by the then President. The aged Father of His Excellency being present, it was made a question, if the President should precede his own father? *By right* as President, yes—by filial courtesy as son, no. Exceptions to ordinary claims of social or even official precedence, may also be allowed by courtesy to strangers of distinction who make us passing visits, to remarkable worth and merit, such as philanthropists and other benefactors of mankind exhibit, or to extraordinary and acknowledged scientific, artistic or literary excellence. Deference to these conditions, illustrate the existence of that advanced state of civilization it is our aim to acquire.

In making visits, always send in, or leave your card. At receptions, the usher takes your card. At other times, the person called upon not being at home, you turn down the right hand upper corner of the pasteboard to indicate that you came in person; and if the visit is intended for the various members of a family, you either give several cards or leave one with the entire right side folded over. The choice is immaterial. When you go away from the city altogether, do not omit to send a card upon which P. P. C. is written on one of the lower corners. A prompt notice should be taken of the first visit received, and when such visit inaugurates an acquaintance, the card or call should be at once honored. An intervening period of three days marks high-breeding, as it evinces your pleasure at forming the acquaintance, so that a return visit, within a day or so, is therefore a delicate compliment. With regard to entertainments, other than the dinner, one is at liberty not to send a written answer of acceptance; but in case of non-acceptance, it is certainly more polite to send a regret. Of course, if an answer is requested (the R. S. V. P. means the same thing), an answer should be given accordingly. When one has a small house, it is important to know what number of guests may be expected, and always more pleasant for a hostess to be thus assured. In making calls, the usual visiting hours are from two until five. This portion of the day is particularly set apart for formal calls. An evening visit implies some degree of social acquaintance, and should never be made as a first call, unless you are invited to come unceremoniously.

Persons in private life, having no official position in Washington, are in a measure exempt from the necessity of making the official round of visits, or of giving large entertainments;

yet any one who enters into general society here, must of course conform to the official rules of precedence and etiquette. Private life here has its advantages as well as its disadvantages. It is pleasant to select your own company, even though choice extend to but a limited number; and the private citizen is free to do this. Washington will certainly become more and more a central social point of attraction to persons of wealth and refinement who can exercise freedom of selection, and who will also add to the already charming variety of society. Such persons must surely appreciate our social advantages over all other cities of the Union.

Young people amongst us have never as a common rule been allowed to tyrannize over society, as they do in New York and in other cities; and the ineffable vulgarity of *coteries* presided over by young ladies, and not dignified by the presence of their seniors, has not, we believe, had much if any encouragement here. Probably the presence of so many personages of importance in the State, assists to keep the young in their proper place. One may here see, what we fear is not so usual elsewhere, young ladies remain standing as they should do, until the mother or married lady may be seated, and at all events an appearance of subordination, which speaks well for the future. Our young people are not often invited to dinners, but left to participate in the simpler forms of gaiety. We have heard it said, that a woman did not enjoy a dinner-conversation, or play a good hand at whist, under thirty!

On New-Year's day, ladies are not expected to make visits. Gentlemen call to pay the compliments of the season, and ladies stay at home to welcome visitors.

We think our ladies make a mistake, and also fatigue themselves unnecessarily, by receiving standing. This is a great tax on the strength, and much more formal than is apt to be agreeable. In very large receptions, a lady who receives can scarcely be seated; but in the usual morning at home, would not our guests remain longer, and be more at ease, if seated in pleasant circles, rather than left standing in formal groups in the middle of the room. Magnetism counts for something the world over, and stiff constraint destroys electric currents.

As to the refreshments proper to provide at a morning reception, the choice is quite optional here, as in other of our cities. A cup of chocolate is however usually offered, and many still preserve the old custom, and add other refreshing drinks and many tempting comfits.

The idea of writing this little pamphlet was first suggested to us by a distinguished personage here, who thought something of the kind would be well received, and ought to be published. The very limited scope we have given ourselves, shows for itself in the size of this little essay; for we have not proposed to attempt the history of social customs since preadamitic periods, nor yet to instruct in all the rules of a manual of good-manners, nor to give the rounded polish of a Chesterfield, but simply to indicate certain peculiarities of Washington society.

We have heard some of the subjects we have just hinted at commented upon from our first acquaintance with official social life here; and although we have alluded to many little matters, which must seem rather puerile and perhaps unworthy of serious attention, yet these are the very questions one asks most often upon first arrival in Washington. We do not endeavor or presume to instruct, but rather desire to recapitulate mooted points, show how troublesome their unsettled condition makes them, and ask for a woman's congress, or "kitchen cabinet," to define them in the interest of society.

So far as we have noted some customs, we have preferred to leave as many more unnoted, on the supposition that our reader forms a "court that knows something."

Etiquette.

Appendix.

As far back as 1825, the President held a levee every other Wednesday evening, and it was customary to make the announcement in the *National Intelligencer.* The hour was at that time from 8 to 10 P. M., and it was usual to offer some refreshments, which were placed on trays, and carried about the rooms by waiters. Gentlemen then appeared in small-clothes, which was the accepted full dress of the period; and we remember hearing our father say that so great was the precision, that although some gentlemen occasionally wore boots, it was considered more proper to go in silk stockings and pumps. Of course the usual dress suit of black has long since taken the place of this more courtly, though less convenient, style of dress. It was not at first the custom to have music—except on New Year's day, when a government band discoursed patriotic airs; but in the time of Mr. Adams, and after the East Room was opened in 1828, music and dancing enlivened these receptions, and splendid suppers were given. So long as such degree of exact form marked these receptions as to assure only the presence of well-bred people of decorous manners, this style of entertainment prevailed; but finally such excesses took place in the greater latitude that was afterward allowed, as to make it unadvisable either to have dancing or to give suppers, except at invited entertainments—but of these, we remember some very memorable and elegant receptions that have been given, on special occasions, at the Executive Mansion.

We desire to append the following letter from John Quincy Adams, written when Secretary of State, and addressed as a private communication to the Vice-President of the United

States. It strikes us that the eminent writer is somewhat illogical when he speaks of the "whole affair" as "of very little importance," while at the same moment he shows by the very subject matter of his letter the "importance" then, as now, of adopting some more fixed and exact code. Until this is done, it will become more and more difficult to avoid misconstructions and unpleasant relations, in a state of society where the social intercourse cannot be separated from official position and its exigencies. Even the public service requires this:

WASHINGTON, DEC. 29, 1819.

The Vice-President of the U. S.

DEAR SIR: It has been suggested to me, that some of the members of the Senate, entertaining the opinion that a formal visit in person or by card is due from each of the executive departments, at the commencement of every session of Congress, to every Senator upon his arrival at the seat of government, have considered the omission on my part to pay such visits, as the withholding from them of a proper mark of respect, or even as implying a pretension to exact such a formality from them. Disclaiming every such pretension and every such claim on my part, I take the liberty of submitting to you the following explanation of the motives which have governed my conduct in relation to this subject.

I have invariably considered the government of the United States as a government for the transaction of business, and that no ceremonial for the mode or order of interchanging visits between the persons belonging to the respective departments in it had ever been established. I was myself five years a member of the Senate, and at four of the five sessions of Congress which I attended, was accompanied at this place by my wife. During that time, I never once received a first visit from any one of the heads of departments, nor did my wife ever receive a first visit from any one of their ladies, except perhaps *once*, when she was sick, from Mrs. Madison. We always called upon them soon after our arrival at Washington, not from any opinion that it was an obligation of duty, but because we understood and believed it to be usual, and because we did not think it improper. We made an exception, after the first session, with regard to Mr. Gallatin, who, never having returned my first visit, was supposed not to incline to that sort of intercourse with us.

When I came to reside at this place, two years since, I was under the impression that the usages, with regard to visiting, were as I had known and practised them ten years before—that, as a member of the administration, I had no sort of claim to a first visit from any member of either house of Congress, but that neither had any member of Congress any claim to a first visit from me—that the interchange and order of visits was entirely optional on both sides, and that no rule of etiquette whatsoever existed, which required that either party should pay the first visit, or indeed any visit, to the other.

In the course of the winter of 1817—18, two members of the Senate, for both of whom I entertained the highest respect, and with one of whom I had had the pleasure of sitting several years in the Senate, called at my office, and informed me that there was a minute of a rule agreed upon, not officially but privately, by the members of the Senate of the first Congress, that the Senators of the United States paid the first visit to no person except the President of the United States. I observed to them, that, as during five years' service as a Senator, I had never seen or heard of this rule, I could hardly consider it as having been much observed; that I could, however, have no possible objection to the Senators prescribing to *themselves* any rule of visiting which they might think proper. But, I asked them if they understood the rule as implying an order that *other persons* should first visit them? They answered, if I recollect right, by no means. And I supposed they viewed the whole affair as I did, that is, of very little importance. I have, therefore, paid no visits of form to members of the Senate; and, although always happy to receive and return the visits of those who pleased to call upon me, and happy to invite to my house every member of the Senate, whether he had or had not paid me a visit, who would give me the honour of his company, I yet always respected the motives of those who declined paying me any visit, or even frequenting my house at all. I exacted nothing from them, which they might think incompatible with their dignity. I presumed they would exact nothing from me, not within the line of my official duty. I soon learned, that, if I should make it a rule to pay the first visit to every Senator at each session, the same compliment would be claimed, if not by all, at least by a large proportion of the members of the House of Representatives; and I could find no republican principle which would, to my own mind, justify me in refusing to the members of one house that which I should yield as due to the members of another. At the commencement of each session, I have visited the presiding member of each house, not from a sense of obligation, but of propriety. I have not felt it my duty to pay first visits to any individual member of either house; nor has it entered my imagination, that a first visit was *due* from any member of either house to me.

If there is a body of men upon earth for whom, more than for any other, I ought to cherish every feeling of attachment, superadded to every sentiment of reverence, it is the Senate of the United States. Its importance and dignity, as one of the branches of the legislature, as one of the component parts of the supreme executive, and as the tribunal of official honour and virtue, cannot be more highly estimated by any man than by me. My father had the honor of being its first presiding officer. I had, for five years, that of being one of its members; and through every successive administration of this government, from the establishment of the national constitution to this time, I have received frequent tokens of its confidence, which can never be obliterated from my memory, and claiming all my gratitude. For every individual member of the body, I feel all the respect due to his public character; and there is not one member towards whom I entertain a sentiment other than that of regard and esteem. If, therefore, the principle upon which I have omitted to pay them first visits of form should ultimately fail of meeting their approbation, it will be serious cause of regret to me; but, at all events, I hope they will impute it to any other cause than intentional disrepect to them.

I take this occasion of observing that, with my approbation and advice, my wife has acted upon the same principle with regard to the ladies connected with members of the Senate or House of Representatives, who have visited this place during the sessions of Congress, that I have pursued in the relation to the members themselves. She has paid no first visits to ladies with whom she had not the advantage of being acquainted. She has received with pleasure, and returned the visits of all ladies who have called upon her, whether connected with members of Congress or otherwise. She has visited her friends on the usual footing of private citizens, without pretension to claim, and without being sensible of any obligation to pay, any first visit. She would have paid, with much pleasure, this compliment to the ladies of members of

Congress, had it been proper, in her opinion, to confine it to them. But she was aware that many other ladies, equally strangers to her, and, though not immediately allied to members of Congress, of character and standing in society equally respectable, occasionally came to spend some time in the city; and knowing it to be impossible that she should visit them all, she declined the invidious task of discriminating whom she should and whom she should not first visit. If, in observing this rule, she has deviated from the practice of some other ladies, in situations similar to her own, she has conformed to that which she constantly observed when she was herself the wife of a Senator at the seat of government. She then always called upon the ladies of the heads of departments when she came to Washington, and always understood it to be the common practice. She lays no claim, however, to the same attention from any other lady; and, having no pretension to visits of etiquette herself, thinks herself amenable to none from others. She has invited to her house, without waiting for formal visits, every lady of a member of Congress to whom she had not reason to believe such an invitation would be unwelcome; and, while feeling it as a favour from those who have accepted her invitations, she has only regretted the more rigorous etiquette of those who have declined, inasmuch as it bereft her of the happiness which she would have derived from a more successful cultivation of their acquaintance. She would regret still more the error which should, in any instance, attribute her conduct to a pretension of any kind on her part, or to a disregard of what is due from her to others.

I have thought this candid explanation of the motives of my conduct particularly due to those members of the Senate who, it has been intimated to me, have thought there was something exceptionable in it. I submit it to your indulgence and to their candour, with the sincere and earnest assurance of my perfect respect for yourself and them.

John Quincy Adams.

www.ingramcontent.com/pod-product-compliance
Lightning Source LLC
LaVergne TN
LVHW011125110826
845150LV00008B/2252
* 9 7 8 1 4 1 8 1 9 5 4 7 2 *